THE WINTER GARDEN

JOHN GALSWORTHY   *Raphael.*

THE WINTER GARDEN

FOUR DRAMATIC PIECES

BY

JOHN GALSWORTHY

WITH A FOREWORD BY
MRS. GALSWORTHY

DUCKWORTH

3 HENRIETTA STREET, LONDON, W.C. 2

First published 1935
(*All rights reserved*)
Copyright in U.S.A.

Made *and* printed *in* Great Britain
By The Camelot Press Ltd
London *and* Southampton

CONTENTS

	PAGE
THE WINTER GARDEN . . .	9
ESCAPE (Episode VII) . . .	31
THE GOLDEN EGGS . . .	39
SIMILES	51

5

FOREWORD

Four short dramatic pieces by John Galsworthy, two complete and two incomplete, all hitherto unpublished, are here assembled.

The first, *The Winter Garden*, a complete one-act play, is of early date ; so far as memory serves, it was written about 1908, the Christmas of which year found us installed in a French Riviera hotel, against a somewhat similar background to that depicted in the play. The result, this very light-hearted young bit of work, was decorated with a sub-title by its author : " A Symphonic Squib," which seems to describe it with perfect accuracy.

The second example, a short and complete scene, belongs to a much later period, that of *Escape*, i.e. 1926. It was discarded from the play by its author as " not advancing the action sufficiently to justify its inclusion " – for his austere taste never would tolerate anything in his work that seemed to him redundant. And so, in spite of the protests, and to the regret, of his critic-in-chief, it was thrown out. I still hold that, as part of an already existing scene, i.e. that of the " Plus Fours " man and wife and following on their exit, it would be in its appropriate place, for it does show a decidedly new angle in Matt Dennant's attitude to his misfortunes, and it is certainly entertaining.

The third example, a fragment, must, I think, have been written in the winter of 1925, or of 1926. Either of those dates would account for the appearance

7

and condition of the thin, golden-yellow, travel-worn paper on which the one scene is written. The glorious winter sun of Arizona or the Christmas-midsummer sun of Cape Colony was surely responsible for the mellowing of the un-English-looking sheets, written out of doors, as always where climate permitted. The play was evidently put aside for more pressing work, and then forgotten. Sad, for Mr. Freville might have afforded us a good deal of amusement ; from the few deft strokes already placed, we get a definite impression of his character.

The fourth example, also a fragment, was written in the autumn of 1932, after the completion of the last novel : *Over the River*. The subject was more or less suggested by the *cause célèbre* which so thrilled our Edwardian days — the case of the Pearl Necklace. . . . This piece of work is very much in the rough, and should not be considered as in any sense shaped to its final form. Its author, a most meticulous workman, would have given it many revisions.

Nevertheless, it has been suggested that this fragment should take its place with the rest ; and that work covering so wide a span of time — from an Early period, through the Middle one, to that Late day when the Great Reaper was already so near — may prove of interest to the student or to the devotee of the English drama of our day.

ADA GALSWORTHY

January 1935

8

THE WINTER GARDEN

A Symphonic Squib

CHARACTERS

SIR GEORGE BLANE	.	G.C.B.
LADY BLANE .	.	His Wife
MISS BLANE .	.	His Daughter
CAPTAIN BLANE	.	D.S.O.
CANON BATH .	.	A Valetudinarian
REV. HANDEL MILDRED .	.	A Sleepless Chaplain
MR. KENEALY .	.	A Scotsman
MR. FITCH .	.	A Silent Solicitor
MRS. FITCH .	.	His Nervous Wife
MRS. CAMPION	.	A Wandering Widow
MRS. BIRD .	.	A Detached Woman
THE HONOURABLE GERTRUDE SLOANEY		A Traveller for Health
MONSIEUR VERT	.	The Hotel Proprietor

THE WINTER GARDEN

*Before the curtain rises a hum of noises is heard,
ending with a violent sneeze.* LADY BLANE'S
voice rises.

LADY BLANE :
Did you get your game, George ?

SIR GEORGE :
What ?

> *There is the sound of another loud shrill
> sneeze ; it is repeated. The curtain rises on*
> CANON BATH'S *third sneeze.*

> *The scene disclosed is the Winter Garden of a
> Riviera hotel in January, greenly caparisoned
> with plants, chairs, rugs, divans, and heated
> with hot air.* MR. *and* MRS. FITCH *are playing
> chess.*

LADY BLANE :
Did you get your game, George ?

SIR GEORGE :
What ? Yes.

MISS BLANE :
Did you win, Dad ?

SIR GEORGE :
Yes. What ?

> CANON BATH *sneezes.*

11

Hon. Gertrude [*sotto voce*] :
That poor old gentleman – it's *rather*——

Sir George :
What ?

Lady Blane : Quite !

 Mr. Kenealy *loudly crackles " The Times," and looks round it over his spectacles. His face is fresh-coloured and bearded, with shrewd eyes.*

Mrs. Bird [*in a soft, sympathetic voice*] :
I'm always so sorry for people who read *The Times* ; such a very loud noise——

Captain Blane :
Ye-e-e-as !

Mrs. Bird :
Don't you think ?

Captain Blane :
Ye-e-e-as !

 Canon Bath *sneezes. All look at him.* Mrs. Campion *rests her knitting and sniffs.*

Hon. Gertrude :
I do think it's *rather*——

Lady Blane :
Quite !

 Mrs. Fitch *titters.*

Rev. Handel :
Er – I tried bromide last night – er——

MISS BLANE :
Oh ! Mr. Mildred, do tell me the effect. [*Whooping*] It's got such a *funny* taste.

REV. HANDEL :
It – er——

SIR GEORGE :
What ?

    CANON BATH *sneezes. The* REV. HANDEL *does not finish his remark.* MRS. BIRD *is talking in a cooing manner to* CAPTAIN BLANE.

CAPTAIN BLANE :
Ye-e-e-as ! Ye-e-e-as ! She's lookin' very seedy ; quite pulled down.

MRS. BIRD [*cooing*] :
Um !

CAPTAIN BLANE :
Ye-e-e-as !

LADY BLANE :
How many holes up were you, George ?

SIR GEORGE :
What ?

    MR. KENEALY *crackles* " The Times " *and looks round it.* MR. FITCH *clears his throat sonorously.*

LADY BLANE :
How many holes up were you, George ?

13

SIR GEORGE :
  Three. What ?

HON. GERTRUDE :
  Oh ! That's *rather*——

LADY BLANE :
  Quite !

CAPTAIN BLANE [*in answer to* MRS. BIRD] :
  Ye-e-e-as !
    MRS. CAMPION *sniffs*.

REV. HANDEL :
  I'm going – er – to try sulphonal to-night.

HON. GERTRUDE :
  That's *rather* daring.

LADY BLANE :
  Quite.

SIR GEORGE :
  What ?

MISS BLANE :
  Mr. Millicent says he's going to try [*whooping*] *sulphonal* to-night.

SIR GEORGE :
  What ?

REV. HANDEL :
  Sulphonal, Sir George ; they say it makes you go off——

    CANON BATH *sneezes*.

14

REV. HANDEL :
Beautifully.

SIR GEORGE :
Sulphonal ?

LADY BLANE :
Quite ! I've tried it.

SIR GEORGE :
What ?

MISS BLANE [*whooping*] :
Mother says she's tried it.

MR. KENEALY *crackles " The Times."*

CAPTAIN BLANE [*in answer to* MRS. BIRD] :
Ye-e-e-as. Had a lot of trouble with his horses. He's a good sort ; ye-e-e-as !

MRS. BIRD [*cooing*] :
Umm !

CAPTAIN BLANE :
Ye-e-e-as !

MR. FITCH *clears his throat.*

REV. HANDEL :
To-morrow night, if sulphonal doesn't oper-ate, I shall – er – try putting my feet in cold water.

MISS BLANE :
Oh ! Mr. Mildred, how *beastly* for them in the middle of the night !

15

SIR GEORGE [*interested*] :
   What ?

   CANON BATH *sneezes.*

HON. GERTRUDE :
   Mr. Mildred says he's going to try cold
water ; it seems *rather*——

LADY BLANE :
   Quite ! Are you going to play to-morrow ?

SIR GEORGE :
   If I can get anyone to come out.

REV. HANDEL :
   I'd play with you, General, if – er——

HON. GERTRUDE [*sotto voce to him*] :
   Oh ! That's rather good of you !

SIR GEORGE :
   What ?

MISS BLANE :
   Mr. Mildred says [*whoops*] he'd play with
you if——

   CANON BATH *sneezes.*

SIR GEORGE [*rubbing his hands*] :
   I'll take him on.

LADY BLANE :
   He can't sleep.

SIR GEORGE :
   Sleep ? Who wants to sleep – what ?

MR. FITCH :
   Check. [*He clears his throat.*]
      MRS. FITCH *titters.* MRS. CAMPION *looks
   at them and sniffs.*
CAPTAIN BLANE [*in answer to* MRS. BIRD] :
   Ye-e-e-as, it would ; ye-e-e-as. What do
you say, Canon Bath ?
CANON BATH [*sneezing*] :
   The climate here is indifferent ; too easterly,
too drying——
MRS. BIRD :
   Umm, umm !
CANON BATH :
   Too localised.
CAPTAIN BLANE :
   Ye-e-e-as.
      CANON BATH *sneezes.*
REV. HANDEL :
   I've tried hay-flower baths, Lady Blane –
they were——
HON. GERTRUDE :
   Oh ! They're *rather*——
MISS BLANE :
   They're so [*whoops*] *beastly* messy.
REV. HANDEL :
   Er – do you know Cannes, Lady Blane ?
LADY BLANE :
   Quite !

17

REV. HANDEL :
Er – I didn't sleep in Cannes——

MR. KENEALY crackles " The Times."
MRS. CAMPION gets up, sniffs, and sits down
again.

SIR GEORGE :
What ?

LADY BLANE :
Will you have your tea, George ?

REV. HANDEL :
Tea keeps me awake all night.

CAPTAIN BLANE [*to* MRS. BIRD] :
Ye-e-e-as. Nice little woman. Ye-e-e-as.
Goes there for her health.

MRS. BIRD [*cooing*] :
Umm, umm !

CAPTAIN BLANE :
Ye-e-e-as. Awf'lly poor health.

MRS. BIRD :
Umm !

CAPTAIN BLANE :
Ye-e-e-as !

CANON BATH :
You were speaking of her health. [*He
sneezes.*]

MRS. CAMPION again gets up, sniffs, and
again sits down. As she resumes her seat,

Mr. Kenealy *crackles " The Times " with desperation. There is a silence.*

Sir George [*suddenly*] :
Never was in such a dull place in my life. What ?

Miss Blane :
I'll go and see if the glass is going up.
She rises, crosses left, and goes out under an arch left forward. Canon Bath *sneezes.*

Sir George :
What ?

Mrs. Bird [*raising her voice*] :
I do think it's so delicious there, don't you, Canon Bath ?

Canon Bath :
There is a prevalence of north wind.

Mrs. Bird :
Umm !

Canon Bath :
The aspect—— [*He sneezes.*]

Captain Blane :
Ye-e-e-as !

Sir George [*suddenly*] :
Will you take me on at chess, Miss Sloaney ? What ?

Hon. Gertrude :
I'm rather afraid——

19

MR. FITCH :
Check. [*He clears his throat.* MRS. FITCH *titters.*]

SIR GEORGE [*with a disgusted movement*] :
Those people have got the men. They've always got 'em. What ?

LADY BLANE :
Your tea's gettin' cold, George. Quite ! [*Re-enter* MISS BLANE, *pleasurably excited. She is followed in a few seconds by* MONSIEUR VERT, *the hotel proprietor, a short square man with a short square beard.*]

MISS BLANE [*whooping*] :
The hotel bus has upset.

SIR GEORGE :
What ?

MISS BLANE :
The hotel bus has [*whooping*] upset !
There are signs of great animation in the Winter Garden, all rising instinctively. MR. *and* MRS. FITCH, *recollecting that they do not know the Blanes, resume their seats in eager but suspended animation ;* MRS. CAMPION *remains standing and still knitting, with her eyes fixed on the group right, which now includes* CAPTAIN BLANE, MRS. BIRD, *and outlying portions of the seated* CANON BATH. MR. KENEALY *regards them above* "*The Times.*"

LADY BLANE :
Here's Monsieur Vert ! Tell me, please.
[MONSIEUR VERT *approaches.*] How did it
happen ?

HON. GERTRUDE [*concerned*] :
It's *rather* dreadful !

CAPTAIN BLANE :
I say, look here, can I do anything – the
horses !

MRS. BIRD :
Oh ! The *poor* horses !

CANON BATH :
Has anybody suffered injury ?

    MONSIEUR VERT *is about to reply.*

SIR GEORGE :
Who was drivin' the d——d thing ?
Drunk, I suppose ! What ?

REV. HANDEL :
Er – was he badly—— ?

SIR GEORGE :
What ?

MRS. BIRD :
Poor man !

LADY BLANE :
Is he *quite*——

MONSIEUR VERT [*speaking for the first time*] :
It is – nodings – it is a she——

SIR GEORGE :
What ?

MRS. CAMPION [*approaching resolutely, disregarding or perhaps remembering the fact that she is not yet within the circle of the Blanes' acquaintance, and producing smelling salts*] :
These are very strong.

MONSIEUR VERT :
It was a she——

CANON BATH *rises with a sneeze.*

SIR GEORGE :
The devil ! I can't hear. What ?

MONSIEUR VERT :
A lady of the town——

SIR GEORGE :
What ?

There is a considerable decrescendo of interest.

LADY BLANE :
Monsieur Vert says a lady of the town was hurt.

SIR GEORGE :
Where ? What ?

MRS. BIRD [*languidly*] :
Poor thing !

CANON BATH :
Very careless. [*He resumes his seat.*]

22

Monsieur Vert [*with some excitement*] :
No, no ; it was nod.   It was a she-dog – a beech——

    Canon Bath *sneezes.*

Sir George :
What ?

Monsieur Vert :
Her leetle dog bit her behind – de leg.

Captain Blane :
Really ? Ha, he ! Ha, ha !

Sir George [*brightening*] :
Leg ? What ?

Mrs. Campion [*to* Sir George, *taking charge
    of the incident*] :
The bus upset, and a Frenchwoman's little dog who was seated in it bit her by the leg.

Lady Blane [*frigidly*] :
Quite ! George, will you have some fresh tea ?

    Mrs. Campion, *with an angry look at*
Lady Blane, *sniffs and retires towards the
settee.*

Hon. Gertrude :
The poor little dog.   It's *rather* hard on it.

Miss Blane :
Poor darling !   I'm sure she frightened it by *squealing*. [*She whoops.*]

CAPTAIN BLANE :
My French fencin' master's dog once saw
him fightin', and took him by the trousers.

HON. GERTRUDE :
Not really !

CAPTAIN BLANE :
Tore them ! Ye-e-e-as !

MRS. BIRD :
Umm !

CAPTAIN BLANE :
Ye-e-e-as !

LADY BLANE [*abruptly*] :
Did the silly woman ill-treat the dog after
it bit her, Monsieur Vert ?

MONSIEUR VERT [*a little surprised*] :
She is blooded !

SIR GEORGE :
What ?

LADY BLANE :
Monsieur Vert says the woman bled.

SIR GEORGE :
Best thing in the world for her. What ?

HON. GERTRUDE :
But the poor little dog—— ?

MISS BLANE :
Where is it ?

MONSIEUR VERT :

It's deeth are sharp.   It ees here somewhere.

LADY BLANE [*decidedly*] :

Frightened out of its wits – poor little thing !

MISS BLANE :

I *must* look after it.   [*She runs off left, followed by* MONSIEUR VERT.]

CANON BATH :

I do not care for foreign dogs.   [*He sneezes.*]

MR. KENEALY *rattles " The Times " angrily, as though to ask for silence.*

SIR GEORGE [*muttering*] :

What an infernal noise !

At this moment a spirited black Toy Pomeranian enters from left, followed by MISS BLANE.

HON. GERTRUDE :

It's *rather* a darling !

CAPTAIN BLANE :

Jolly little beggar – ye-e-e-as !

MRS. BIRD :

Sweet !

LADY BLANE :

Quite !

MRS. CAMPION *sniffs.   There is a movement towards the dog, which is captured.   They surround the dog, and stare at it.*

MISS BLANE :
It's hungry.

CANON BATH :
Don't put it near *my* legs, please.

MISS BLANE :
It wouldn't hurt a fly. Would you, *darling*?
[*She kisses its nose.*]

 Re-enter MONSIEUR VERT *from left.*

MONSIEUR VERT :
De lady wishes her leedle daug.

 *There is a silence, marked by resentment on
the ladies' faces.*

LADY BLANE [*decisively*] :
Has she got over her hysteria ?

MISS BLANE [*whooping*] :
Oh ! Not yet ! I want to *feed* it ! Can't
you say it's run away ?

HON. GERTRUDE [*with a smile*] :
That's *rather* daring !

LADY BLANE :
Will you guarantee that she won't ill-use it,
Monsieur Vert ?

SIR GEORGE :
Let him have the tyke ! What ?

MISS BLANE :
Father !

26

MONSIEUR VERT :
De lady——

CAPTAIN BLANE :
Look here – is it a bad bite ? I know something about bites.

MONSIEUR VERT :
She haf nod showed me ; it is close by de knee. [MRS. CAMPION *sniffs*.]

CAPTAIN BLANE [*smoothing his moustaches*] :
I see – ye-e-e-as !

LADY BLANE :
Silly woman !

MONSIEUR VERT :
I will take de daug, plese.

CANON BATH :
It will be better to allow Monsieur to take the dog.

REV. HANDEL :
Er – I think – perhaps——

MISS BLANE :
Oh ! but – Mr. Mildred, if she [*whooping*] *beats* it——

HON. GERTRUDE :
That would be *rather* dreadful !

MONSIEUR VERT :
Plese to let me haf de daug, Mees.

MRS. CAMPION [*coming resolutely forward*] :
I will take the dog to her, and see that she
does not ill-treat it.

> LADY *and* MISS BLANE, *the* HON. GER-
> TRUDE *and* MRS. BIRD *gaze at her with
> incipient toleration. With a look round of
> bland ingratiation* MRS. CAMPION *takes the
> dog from* MISS BLANE *and proceeds left,
> followed by* MONSIEUR VERT.

LADY BLANE :
Quite !

HON GERTRUDE :
It's *rather* sweet of her !

CAPTAIN BLANE :
Ye-e-e-as !

MISS BLANE :
I must go too.

> *She*, CAPTAIN BLANE, *and* MRS. BIRD
> *follow in a line. The remaining occupants of
> the Winter Garden sink back into the precise
> attitudes they occupied at the opening of the
> scene. There is a silence of some seconds.*

SIR GEORGE :
Never was in such a dog-hole in my life !

LADY BLANE :
Will you have some fresh tea, George ?
This is cold – quite.

SIR GEORGE :
What ? [*There is another silence.*]

REV. HANDEL [*sidling towards* LADY BLANE *on the divan*] :
Er – I'm very much afraid – that I shan't sleep to-night, after this – er——

As he reaches the word " to-night *" re-enter quickly* MISS BLANE, MRS. CAMPION, MRS. BIRD, *and* CAPTAIN BLANE *in a line. And Simultaneously*

HON. GERTRUDE :
That's *rather*——

LADY BLANE :
Quite !

MISS BLANE [*beginning with a whoop*] :
I say——

CAPTAIN BLANE [*in answer to a sentence of* MRS. BIRD'S] :
Ye-e-e-as !

MRS. BIRD :
Ummm !

MRS. CAMPION *sniffs.*

SIR GEORGE [*who has nodded off, with tremendous vehemence*] :
What ?

29

Canon Bath *discharges an enormous sneeze.*

Mr. Fitch *clears his throat with special loudness.*

Mrs. Fitch *titters shrilly.*

Mr. Kenealy *hits " The Times " a fearful blow, which makes it crackle to the soul.*

Suddenly, as if startled by this chord of sound, all are silent, and look at each other.

The Curtain *falls.*

Circa 1908.

1926

ESCAPE

EPISODE VII
THE FOXHUNTER

ESCAPE

Episode VII

An hour has passed. A road on the edge of the moor. MATT, who has been kneeling by his car, which has broken down, raises himself to see the figure of a dismounted FOXHUNTER coming towards him.

FOXHUNTER :
Engine trouble ? [MATT *nods*.] Well, she hasn't got away from you, like my beast. Come across a mare loose ?

MATT :
Afraid not.

FOXHUNTER :
Never rains but it pours. Positively first car I've met, and lo ! she's in trouble.

MATT [*taking in the* FOXHUNTER, *who is obviously a young man of his own species*] :
Seen the convict, Sir ?

FOXHUNTER :
No ; but they've all been keeping their eyes peeled.

MATT :
Aha ! So have I.

33

FOXHUNTER [*with some distaste*] :
Not a pastime I care for – shan't view-halloa
if *I* see him.

MATT :
Why not ?   Can't have desperadoes loose
on the moor.   Safety first !

FOXHUNTER :
But this poor devil's a gentleman.

MATT :
Nothing like a gentleman for being unsafe.

FOXHUNTER [*with increasing displeasure*] :
What !   Poor draggled brute with the whole
pack at his heels – dangerous !

MATT [*grinning*] :
Fox at bay !

FOXHUNTER :
Fox we killed to-day was digested in two
minutes by my watch.

MATT :
Have hounds gone home ?

FOXHUNTER :
Yes ;   they went on over.   Mare unshipped
me at the edge of a bog – went in plump, and
got away while I was collecting myself.

MATT [*eyeing mudstains*] :
I see.   Well, I'd change places with you.

34

[*Gazing at car*] This is the least attractive Ford I ever drove.

FOXHUNTER :
Your own ?

MATT :
No ; belongs to some friends. They said I might take a run on the moor and look for the convict.

FOXHUNTER :
Good for the convict ! Been fishing too ?

MATT :
No. Camouflage.

FOXHUNTER [*with increasing displeasure*] :
Gosh ! You really are out man-hunting ?

MATT :
I say – *you're* not the convict, by any chance ?

FOXHUNTER :
I ? What the——? My good Sir, should I tell you, if I were ?

MATT :
M'm, no ! Forgive my asking. But they always change their clothes first thing, and yours are so priceless. You could get out of Abraham's bosom in that rig.

35

FOXHUNTER [*eyeing* MATT *with suspicion*] :
Look here ! What made you ask that damn fool question ?

MATT :
Well – your sympathy with him. You're about his size and appearance too, judging from the papers. And a soldier-man into the bargain, if I'm any judge.

FOXHUNTER [*hastily*] :
Quite right ! And that's why I dislike a fellow-soldier being harried by seedy-looking blokes in Ford flivvers.

MATT [*goggling*] :
Masterly description ; got me where I live, as the Yanks say. Still, a foxhunter's togs are as good as a passport any day, and you've got 'em on.

FOXHUNTER [*dangerously*] :
Are you looney ? Or merely trying to be funny ?

MATT [*suddenly serious*] :
Do you really want that convict chap to get off ?

FOXHUNTER :
What's your game, my friend ? [*Staring hard*] Are you a 'tec ?

MATT :

No. [*Slowly*] I'm the convict. Change clothes with me ! In your togs I could get through.

FOXHUNTER [*completely taken aback*] :

I say ! But – but——

MATT [*with a sad little smile*] :

It's all right. I *am* the convict, but I was only kidding you about the change. Thanks for your sympathy though. You don't know what it means. You'd better get on now. I'm going to take cover again.

FOXHUNTER [*uncertainly – looking from his garments to* MATT] :

But look here – if you mean that you really——

MATT :

No, no ! Too thick ! Accessory and all that. If you could drive that flivver away, though, you'd do me a good turn. But you can't, I'm afraid ; she's bust her vitals. Well, I must do my bunk now. Hope you'll catch your mare. You might say you saw someone like me going up that way.

FOXHUNTER :

You've winded me ; I don't know what to say – it's a knock-out. Well, anyway, you can rely on me.

MATT :

I know.   Sojer to sojer !   So long !   [*He vanishes.*]

FOXHUNTER [*to himself*] :

Gee-hovah !   That's a rum go !

1926.

THE GOLDEN EGGS

FROM AN UNFINISHED PLAY

THE GOLDEN EGGS

ACT I

In his comfortable study, which looks out over the Regent's Park, AUGUSTUS FREVILLE (Gus), well-groomed, and perhaps fifty, is divided between the desire to smoke his morning cigar, and the feeling that anything so nice is inappropriate to his frequently remembered anxiety. He fidgets from the open window to the closed door of the drawing-room, where the specialist is interviewing "poor Blanche." He takes the cigar from a box on a table well-stocked with papers and periodicals, and nicks it absent-mindedly. Really! This is an intolerable business—this dreadful weakness of poor dear Blanche—intolerably anxious—quite intolerably! And a beautiful morning—delightfully sunny! Everything coming out in the Park. The lilac! Ah! Delicious! He interrupts his sniff to listen, and murmurs to himself:

FREVILLE :

Intolerable—this waiting ! Poor Blanche !

He drums his fingers on the table, and the matches catch his eye. He strikes one, and lo ! —the cigar is lighted ! Delicious first draw ! Delicious ! A sound—he puts the cigar behind his back, recoiling to the window, whence a gesture will dispose of it. Nothing ! He smokes. The birds ! The spring birds – delightful ! He murmurs :

Jolly little beggars ! That thrush ! Delicious ! Tt – tt ! Poor Blanche ! Damn that doctor – why doesn't he come out ? [*He takes a letter from his pocket and quizzically regards it ; brushes back his fair grizzled hair complacently.*] Poor Flo ! [*Begins whistling " When the heart of a man," but, suddenly remembering that he is very anxious, looks at the drawing-room door, ceases to whistle, and sighs heavily.*] This is really—— [*Abruptly he puts his cigar into his mouth, and the letter back into his pocket ; advances half way to the drawing-room door, suddenly sees it opening, and stops – his face long, and his cigar behind him, the picture of perfectly sincere apprehension.*] Well, doctor ?

The specialist – grey, clean-shaved, rather bald, with pince-nez, and a docketing eye, has turned to close the door ; FREVILLE, *about to throw the cigar out of the window, has not quite time.*

DOCTOR [*advancing from the door*] :

My dear Mr. Freville – the poor dear lady is most plucky – most plucky.

FREVILLE :

I know, I know. But *how* is she ?

42

DOCTOR :

So plucky that it's difficult to get anything from her, but [*he shakes his head*] – cardiac condition – I'm sorry, but there's only one word for it. [FREVILLE *instinctively covers his ears.*] Yes, yes – but I'm afraid we must face it – alarming. She might – she might fall dead at any moment.

FREVILLE :

Good God !

DOCTOR :

There is just this about it – the thing has never yet been taken seriously. Er – what age is she, Mr. Freville ?

FREVILLE :

Forty-eight.

DOCTOR :

Precisely. With ladies one likes that little point corroborated. Comparatively young – the arteries – still elastic. Nauheim might do wonders for her, yet.

FREVILLE :

Nauheim – in Germany ?

DOCTOR :

It has that misfortune, but what they don't know there about the heart is not known. I haven't alarmed her ; she must not be alarmed.

FREVILLE :

You can't alarm Blanche about *herself*. She never thinks about herself at all.

DOCTOR :

Quite – I'm sure – very sweet woman.

FREVILLE :

My God ! But what is it ?

DOCTOR :

The technical word wouldn't convey much to you, I'm afraid. But it comes to this – some sudden excitement, some extra strain, and the heart might give out with no more warning than a cigar gives you when it stops drawing. [FREVILLE *gives a furtive look at the cigar in his hand.*]

FREVILLE :

But – but we'd no idea. Invalidish, anæmic, all that, but this is utterly beyond anything——

DOCTOR :

That is not uncommon. It's part of the tragedy of these cases. The thing should have been taken in hand much earlier, but even as it is, with care and the Nauheim treatment, I don't see why she shouldn't see sixty yet. As I say, the great thing is not to alarm her – to keep her from worry and excitement, and to get her to Nauheim at once.

44

FREVILLE [*distracted*] :

Yes, yes ! Of course ! Look here, doctor, do you mind telling my son and daughter ? I – positively – I don't feel up to it. Did you mention the heart to my wife ?

DOCTOR :

I told Mrs. Freville she was so run down that there was a certain sluggishness we should have to get rid of.

FREVILLE :

We're not to go beyond that ? All right – all right – only—— Good God !

DOCTOR :

Quite ! But while there's life – I could tell you of a case very similar – and she went on – she went on, I think, nineteen years before she – er – went off. Heart disease is extraordinarily varied, Mr. Freville ; that's what makes it so extremely interesting. I knew another case – he was in the Blues ; one of his valves was practically a passenger. I gave him six months of a quiet life – do you know – that fellow gave me the shock of my life ; he went through the war.

FREVILLE :

Did he ? Splendid ! And you think my wife might——

45

DOCTOR [*with a smile*] :

Mr. Freville, in these cases we hope for the best and er – prepare for the worst. I am ordering her digitalis ; but the great thing first and last is Nauheim. For heart, and eye treatment, nothing like Germany, I'm afraid.

FREVILLE :

Oh ! Germany – it's all the same to me ; but – er – there's the journey ! Surely——

DOCTOR :

A little oscillation is no bad thing in such a case. Don't worry about that, Mr. Freville. Keep her warm and well fed, but lightly – lightly ; for stimulant a thimbleful of brandy now and then ; no heavy wines. A leetle cup of black coffee with sugar – sugar is alcohol – twice a day, will assist. The dear lady is so little concerned about herself, that we must help her, Mr. Freville ; we must help her.

FREVILLE [*with his hand to his head*] :

I should think so. She is – well, I can't tell you what she is to us all.

DOCTOR :

I'm sure, I'm sure. The presence in the house ; the bird that lays the golden eggs. Quite ! By the way, I rather advise celibacy.

FREVILLE [*rolling his eyes*] :

Yes, yes, yes, yes. As a matter of fact – er——

46

DOCTOR [*after pausing for a finish that does not come*] :
Tell me one thing. Are you aware of any complex ? [*Smiling*] Without laying stress on the new cult, we – er – are not above accepting a wrinkle, Mr. Freville.

FREVILLE :
D'you mean was she startled before she was born, or something of that sort ?

DOCTOR [*still smiling*] :
A leetle extreme. But has she any obsession, any pet alarm of any kind ?

FREVILLE :
I don't think so. She's very placid ; always has been.

DOCTOR :
Um ! – Yes. Sometimes, you know, we have a mask to deal with. The more seemingly placid the greater the agitation ; especially in these – er – selfless natures. Anything in the birth of her children – any domestic shock ?

FREVILLE :
Only me, doctor.

DOCTOR [*with a little laugh*] :
Very good ! You have a son and a daughter ? They don't give anxiety ?

47

FREVILLE :
No-o ! They're – modern.

DOCTOR [*dubiously*] :
I see. And – er – where shall I find them ?

FREVILLE :
In the dining-room. I'll show you. It's tremendously good of you, doctor. You can put it so much better than I can. I'm absolutely upset.

DOCTOR :
Don't let it appear, Mr. Freville. We must manage her, as the French say. I should like to see her again, when you come back from Nauheim.

FREVILLE [*laying an envelope on the table*] :
Of course, of course ! [*He turns to a door on the left. The* DOCTOR, *as in a dream, pockets the envelope, and follows.*]

DOCTOR [*looking out of the window*] :
A charming position you have ! This is the best month in London, I always think.

They go out, but almost immediately FREVILLE *returns.*

FREVILLE [*to himself – at the table*] :
Good God – not to alarm her. Not to alarm her. [*He takes a cigar, nicks, lights it, and takes a good long whiff or two, closing his eyes ; then*

48

goes to the drawing-room door and opens it.]
Well, darling ?   How did you like him ?

    BLANCHE FREVILLE *comes in with three
roses and three carnations in a little jar.   She
is a very fragile woman, with a sweet, if slightly
ironic, smile, extremely like what the doctor has
called " a presence in the house."*

BLANCHE :
Oh !   Quite nice for a doctor.   Here's a
clove pink for you, Gus.   [*She pins it into his
buttonhole.*]   Would you like a marrow-bone
at dinner ?

FREVILLE [*carried away by the scent of the clove
    and the thought of marrow-bone*] :
Wouldn't I?   Bless you !   [*Taking her by
the ephemeral shoulders*] He thinks you're
dreadfully run down.

BLANCHE :
My dear, they always do.   It's the hobby
of doctors.   *Parlons d'autres choses.*   What are
you going to do this afternoon ?

FREVILLE [*sidelong*] :
Well, I – er – rather thought of going to
see some Chinese lacquer at the British
Museum.   We're publishing a book on it,
you know.

BLANCHE [*with a look that he does not see, indul-
    gent, half-whimsical, half-malicious*] :

49

That'll be very nice. Perfect day for lacquer. The light is exquisite.

FREVILLE :

That fellow says that Nauheim would buck you up, Blanche. One ought to do what they suggest, don't you think ?

BLANCHE :

My dear, he's given me some stuff ; I think that's indulging him quite enough.

FREVILLE :

That's naughty.

BLANCHE [*quizzical*] :

Are you so anxious to go to Nauheim ?

FREVILLE :

I ? I'm anxious that you should go. It might be a little difficult for me to get away just yet. But Nonny could take you, and I could join you there. Or Roger – he gets ten days at Whitsuntide.

BLANCHE :

My dear, I think you'll all be happier at home. These places are no catch. Nauheim sounds particularly dull. They have to suggest something, you know.

FREVILLE :

That's true, of course. But still, anything that'll do you good !

.   .   .   .

1925 or 1926.

SIMILES

AN UNFINISHED PLAY IN THREE ACTS

CHARACTERS

JOHN BARLEY	.	A Hairdresser
MR. JONES	.	His Victim
MONA CURTIS	.	A Face and Hand Specialist
ARTHUR LEPPEDGE	.	A Stockbroker
HELEN LEPPEDGE	.	His Wife
CADGMAN	.	A Taxi Driver
MR. FROLLING	.	A Pawnbroker
WALSH	. . .	The Leppedges' Maid

ACT I

MADAME LILA'S *hairdressing establishment. The men's room. Thursday, 12.30 noon.*

ACT II

The LEPPEDGES' *flat near the Albert Hall. Thursday, 12.45 noon.*

ACT III

The same. Friday morning.

Kensington, early August. Time : The present.

ACT I

The men's hairdressing room in MADAME LILA'S
*hairdressing establishment in Kensington. It is
not a large affair, and is fitted with three basins
and the usual appurtenances. One assistant
is on his holiday, another is at his lunch, the
third and chief assistant,* JOHN BARLEY, *is at
work on* MR. JONES, *who is lathered up to the
eyes.* JOHN BARLEY *is a shortish stocky man
with a hardwood face and toothbrush moustache.*

BARLEY [*stropping a razor*] :
I've never seen an 'orse race, but I can pick
winners all right.

MR. JONES [*struggling a little with the lather*] :
How do you do it ?

BARLEY [*regarding him – razor suspended*] :
I'm not bothered with appearances. Some
see an 'orse – think it looks pretty and go and
back it. All 'orses look pretty when they're
slicked up. There used to be a song : " The
women, I am told " – and then a line endin' in
" old " – " for catchin' men 'ave many a tricky
way – they've a colour like the rose – but when
that colour goes – 'ow different they look by
light o' day." [*Approaching the upper lip with
the razor and nipping the nostrils*] Not up, I
suppose ?

Mr. Jones [*nasally*] :
  No.

Barley [*shaving*] :
  What we get shaved for, I don't know.
Naturally a mass of 'air – I read in *Tit-Bits* or
was it *John Bull* ? – all the same so far as
accuracy goes – that if the nation stopped
shavin' – million adults, allowin' for beavers –
there'd be an 'undred million minutes a day
saved. One million six 'undred and sixty-six
thousand, six 'undred and six hours a day, or say
nine million hours a week – nine by fifty – four
'undred and fifty million labour hours a year –
all gone down the drain, to make us look pretty.
[*Finishes the upper lip, and pauses.*] They say
that would build four 'undred and fifty new
St. Paulses every year. Or put it another way :
The working day is three 'undred and sixty
minutes. Ten minutes added to that would
throw another man out of every thirty-six on the
dole. We'd all be cave men and there'd be two
'undred and fifty thousand extra unemployed.
Look at the Arabs – all beavers and all unemployed. But all this beautification ! These
red nails the women are goin' in for – d'you
like 'em ?

Mr. Jones :
  No.

54

BARLEY :

Why make 'em red when they're naturally
pink ?

MR. JONES :

Exactly !

BARLEY :

And look at 'air lotions. Gloss ! First you
shampoo the gloss off, and then you stick it on
again ! Why not keep your natural oil ?
What about Absalom or Lady Godiva, or Merlin
or Elijah ? The ravens came and nested in 'is
beard.

MR. JONES :

No, no ; they fed him.

BARLEY :

The Old Testament. Was it 'im who went
up in a chariot of fire ? Or Elisha ? Very like,
those two. All these old tales, nursery rhymes.
I'm thankful I wasn't brought up at my
mother's knee.

MR. JONES :

But about those winners ?

BARLEY :

You want to know my system ? I go on the
fact that they're all crooks except the 'orses.

MR. JONES [*shocked*] :

What ?

BARLEY :

Lord Blankey and the other dukes that 'ave got nothin' to gain – d'you think they're allowed to race straight ? Too many o' these trainers and jockeys an' stable 'ands about 'em. If you know a man's rock-bottom honest, you've got 'im.

MR. JONES :

Cynical that, isn't it ?

BARLEY :

I keep my eyes open ; never believe what I'm told. Take the daily papers. You don't believe 'em, do you ?

MR. JONES :

Not always.

BARLEY :

Better never.

MR. JONES :

What – *The Watch* ?

BARLEY :

Watch ! – You can believe *The Watch* when the news doesn't go against its interests. *The Watch* maintains the stettis quo. You can't trust any paper to give both sides full value. A man stands up for 'imself. 'Tisn't 'is business to keep 'is opponent on 'is feet. Shave be'ind the ears ?

56

MR. JONES :
No.

BARLEY :
Some people abuse the papers ; I don't.
There might be something to be said for
juggin' the lot ; but short o' that you must
take 'em as they come.

MR. JONES :
Do you ever read *The Watch* ?

BARLEY :
Not to say read. Take it up once in a while
when it's left in the Tube. Always the same.
While I trim your 'air, would you like your
'ands seen to, Mr. Jones ?

MR. JONES :
The same girl that did them last time ?

BARLEY :
Miss Curtis. I'll see if she's free.

    He goes to the door at back. MR. JONES
thoughtfully fingers his chins. BARLEY *returns.*

BARLEY :
Comin' in a minute.

MR. JONES [*touching his back hair*] :
There's too much just here.

BARLEY :
Ah ! You won't grow any more on the top.
You've got to the stettis quo there. Anne
Domine.

MR. JONES [*with a slight wry smile*] :
Had your holiday ?

BARLEY [*aproning him*] :
Always take it early September ; better
fishin' then. It's sport makes life worth livin'.
[*Goes for neck clippers.*]

MR. JONES :
Others think work, I believe ; others think
women.

BARLEY [*grinning*] :
Work ? Well, you've got to work if you
want to eat. But women ? Work and women
cancel each other out. Sport's the only real
thing.

MR. JONES :
Fishermen's stories, for instance ?

BARLEY :
'Eard of the man 'oo's wife 'ad a baby ?
'E'd been listenin' to fishermen's stories and
someone asked 'im when 'e was goin' fishin'
'imself. 'E shook 'is 'ead an' said : " No ;
my wife's just 'ad a baby." " What weight ? "
said the other. . . . " Twenty-four pound." . . .
But you've 'eard it ?

MR. JONES :
Yes.

BARLEY :

Um ! Those chestnuts are very artificial.
[*Runs the clipper up the neck.*]

MR. JONES [*wincing*] :

Those clippers are real enough ; and so's
my hair.

BARLEY :

You've been touchin' this with a razor.

MR. JONES :

The edges – yes.

BARLEY [*taking up his scissors and snapping
them*] :

Just a trim, I suppose. [*Swings* MR. JONES
full face.]

> MONA CURTIS *enters ; a pretty girl, carry-
> ing her equipment, and looking pale. She draws
> up a stool, sits on it, and takes one of* MR.
> JONES'S *hands.* BARLEY *snips. A silence.*

MR. JONES :

What do you think of that expression :
" Straight from the horse's mouth " ?

BARLEY [*with a little dry laugh*] :

American. 'Ome of advertisement an' sky-
scrapers. I 'ad an American in yesterday.
Very bitter about stocks an' shares. [*He
suspends the scissors.*] Before the crisis, 'e said,
there 'adn't been an issue of capital for years
over there that 'ad the slightest relation to

reality. I forget 'ow 'e put it – somethin' like the brokers reachin' down the glory, an' waterin' the stock out o' the wells of their imaginations. Same over 'ere, you know. The front they put on some o' these issues – all face-aid.

He goes on snipping, and MONA *pauses a second to give him a faintly smiling look.*

Look at Kreuger – there was a bluff ! Took everybody in – includin' himself.

MR. JONES :

Took me in all right.

BARLEY :

All done by charm, they say. Enjoyed 'isself an' then – pop ! – an' left 'em all in the soup. If the truth was known nothin's worth its market valyer. . . . Think that's enough off, Mr. Jones ? 'Ave a look be'ind. [*Holding a hand mirror to the back hair.*]

MR. JONES :

Yes, I think.

BARLEY :

Flowers and 'oney ? [*Taking up the bottle*] There's an example. You could sell anything with that name. [*To* MONA] What 'ave you got there ? Sweet almond paste ! 'Oo could resist that ? It's all in a name. Look at that Golden 'Air colt last year. Change 'is name

an' he gets rheumatism. [*Sprinkling* Mr.
Jones's *head*] Machine or 'and brush ?

Mr. Jones :
Just comb it, please ; back all round.

Barley :
You're right. D'you think I'd 'ave one of
these brushes on my 'ead ? They're fresh-
washed, of course. [*Combs the hair.*] That
right ? [Mr. Jones *nods.*] While you're
'avin' your 'ands finished, you'll like me to
see what Captain Jinks is tippin' for to-day.

*He goes over to a corner where on a table
are three or four newspapers.*

Mr. Jones [*to the girl*] :
Had a busy week ?

Mona :
Pretty good – considering.

Mr. Jones :
You look as if you wanted a holiday.

Mona :
So I do.

Mr. Jones :
Feeling the heat ?

Mona :
It's my nerves.

Mr. Jones :
D'you know what you remind me of ?

MONA :
No.

MR. JONES :
A tobacco flower. [*At her look of surprise*]
You know them ? Very charming, pale, smell
sweet, but inclined to flop.

MONA [*with a rather sickly smile*] :
Now the other hand, please.

BARLEY [*returning*] :
'Ere you are ! Silverside for the three o'clock,
and Pop goes for the four-thirty. I don't
think you'll better that, to-day.

MR. JONES :
I shan't try. I see now how you spot your
winners.

BARLEY :
Study the papers, and get to learn which o'
the tipsters 'as been out o' luck – then follow
'im.

MR. JONES :
And drop him ?

BARLEY :
When 'e drops you. 'E won't be long.
Some people like an 'orse's name. Some take
a fancy to a jockey, or a trainer, or even an
owner. I've heard of men only bettin' on
Fridays. No use. A tipster 'as got to be
right now and then, or 'e'd lose 'is job. Just

men like you an' me, makin' their livin'. Watch
for 'im to 'ave a losin' sequence, then at his first
winner follow 'im. They don't 'ide their lights
under bushels – these captains – Captain This
and Captain That and Captain The Other –
never get beyond the rank of captain. There
was a major once, but 'e called 'imself " The
General." Military rank ! Every profession
'as its face-aid. Never believe an 'airdresser
'oo says your 'air'll grow again ; you might as
well believe in these artificial pearls.

    MONA *drops the hand she is working on,*
gives a jerk, and takes the hand up again.

MR. JONES :
    If I've got time I'll test your theory. When
I go racing I like to back my own judgment.

BARLEY [*shaking his head*] :
    No ; even the 'orse knows more than you do.
Then there's all these poker-faced fellows waitin'
to take you in.

MR. JONES [*to* MONA] :
    Well, thank you. That seems a good hand,
now. [*He regains possession of it and gets out of*
his chair.] How much will that be altogether ?

BARLEY :
    Ninepence the shave – shillin' the 'air – two
shillin's the 'ands – three and nine. [*Receiving*
five shillings] Thank you.

63

MR. JONES :

Good morning ! [*To* MONA] Good morning ! [*Receives his hat and goes.*]

BARLEY :

I didn't offend 'im, did I ? 'E couldn't
think of an answer – that was it. Nice man.
[*Putting his basin to rights.*]

MONA [*stopping at the door*] :

Mr. Barley——

BARLEY :

I can always talk to 'im. Modest – except
about 'is judgment. Funny 'ow racing goes
to a man's 'ead.

MONA :

Mr. Barley——

BARLEY :

Eh !

MONA :

I'm in trouble.

BARLEY :

Nothin' old-fashioned, I 'ope.

MONA [*coming from the door*] :

No. But I don't know what to do.

BARLEY :

Not unusual.

MONA :

There's a lady – Mrs. Leppedge——

BARLEY :

Ah ! A bright bit – good deal of face-aid about 'er.

MONA :

She's pretty.

BARLEY :

Matter o' taste. Well ?

MONA :

She was in yesterday afternoon.

BARLEY :

Repairs and redecorations.

MONA :

She had her face and neck creamed and massaged. And when she'd gone I saw she'd left her pearls.

BARLEY :

Mocks.

MONA :

Oh, no ! Real pearls.

BARLEY :

You can't tell.

MONA :

These were real. If they hadn't been I wouldn't have done what I did.

BARLEY [*eyeing her pallor*] :

Well ! What did you do ? Tell Madame Lila ?

65

MONA :

I didn't notice them at first. Then I took them up and felt them, and that gave me the idea – so silky ! I just slipped my scarf over them, in case she should come back for them. But she didn't, and I thought : " Well, now she can't do anything till the shop opens to-morrow morning." So I made believe they were in a drawer where I could find them in the morning, and – and I took them away with me.

BARLEY :

What for ?

MONA :

I was going to a dance, and my young man was to be there, and I thought I'd wear them just for that evening. You do get sick of similes, don't you ?

BARLEY :

Can't say – never 'ad any.

MONA :

They did suit me ! But when I got home and put my hand up to my neck, they weren't there.

BARLEY :

Pinched ?

MONA [*distressed*] :

I don't know. It's awful, Mr. Barley.

What am I to do ?   I can't go asking openly about them, because they weren't mine.   If Madame Lila plumps it out at me, I'll never be able to bluff her.   There was nobody but me in the room where Mrs. Leppedge was attended to.

BARLEY :

No enquiry this morning ?

MONA :

Not yet.   But I'm dead scared.   Who's going to believe I took them just to wear at a dance ?

BARLEY :

Anyone who knows women, and that's not many.   What d'you want me to do – believe you ?

MONA :

I hardly slept all night, and whenever I woke up I wished I was dreaming.

BARLEY :

If they was reel (and if they wasn't she'd pretend they was), what should you say they was worth ?

MONA :

Oh – I don't know ; a thousand pounds or more.

BARLEY :

Been round to where you were dancin' ?

MONA :
Yes.   Nothing's been picked up.
BARLEY :
Who's your young man ?
MONA :
Cortin and Cozens.
BARLEY :
Electric light fittin's.   'Im ?
MONA :
Haven't had a chance ; and I wouldn't like him to know.
BARLEY :
Given to practical jokes ?
MONA :
No.
BARLEY :
Where'd you leave him last night ?
MONA :
At my door – he took me home.
BARLEY :
Did he notice the pearls ?
MONA :
Yes ; he said you'd think they were real.
BARLEY :
Why should this woman pitch on you ?
MONA :
I took the pearls off her neck.

68

BARLEY :

She might 'ave done a dozen things after she left here. I should say she couldn't be certain.

MONA :

She took a taxi from the door, and I heard her say " Albert Hall Mansions," and I know that's where she lives.

BARLEY :

Dropped 'em in the cab – that's what she did. It's not for you to accuse yourself. Wait till someone does it for you.

MONA :

I wish I'd never seen the wretched things.

BARLEY [*beckoning to her*] :

You look me in the face. Are you makin' a case for yourself, or tellin' the truth ?

MONA :

Telling the truth.

BARLEY :

Well, don't you do it to anyone else. It can be used against you. You sit tight. It's early closin' to-day. Twelve forty-five already. Where's Madame ?

MONA :

Gone to Gustave's about a transformation.

69

BARLEY :

Ash-blonde, I suppose. This sunburn – women are crazy now to be what they aren't.

MONA :

Mr. Barley, d'you think I might pretend it's one o'clock ?

BARLEY :

I shouldn't. Put a face on it. They've got no evidence. You sit down an' give yourself a touch o' sunburn. You look like a ghost.

MONA :

Sunburned ghost [*with a ghostly laugh*].
    The telephone rings.
Oh ! Oh ! I can't. Mr. Barley.

BARLEY :

It's probably Madame to say she won't be back.

MONA :

No ; I can't. Mr. Barley, quick, or the girl will be coming.

BARLEY :

All right, all right ! [*Moves to the telephone.*] Just stand by. [*He takes up the receiver.*] 'Allo ! . . . Ye-es – Madame Lila's. 'Oo is it ? Leppedge ? [*Gives* MONA *a look.*] Mrs. – Mrs. Leppedge – ye-es ? . . . No, Madame's out. . . . Won't be back – early closin' to-day. . . . 'Oo's speakin' ? Barley – 'ead assistant –

men's department. . . . 'Old the line a minute.
[*Covering the phone – to* Mona] She wants the
girl that did her face and neck yesterday.

Mona :
Oh !

Barley :
Don't dither – don't dither ! Shall I say
you're out ?

Mona :
Yes – no.

Barley :
Well, which ? They ain't the same.

Mona :
Oh ! Advise me, Mr. Barley !

Barley :
Say you'll 'ave a look, and if you can't find
'em, you'll let her know. 'Ere, come to the
phone. [Mona *approaches, and he transfers
the receiver to her.*]

Mona :
Yes, Madam ? . . . [*Listening*] Really,
Madam ?

Barley [*sotto voce*] :
Put some pep in it.

Mona [*louder*] :
Yes, Madam. Shall I have a look round ?
. . . Yes, I seem to remember taking them off ;

but are you sure you didn't put them on, after-
wards ? . . . Really, Madam, I don't think it's
possible they could have been left.

BARLEY :

That's better. Rub it in.

MONA :

Let me have a look round, Madam. What
is your number ? . . . Kensington 80 – 00 – 0.
Yes, Madam. [*She abandons the receiver, and
puts her hand to her heart.*]

BARLEY :

Well, you needn't look for 'em ; that's one
thing. We can spend the time inventin' the
best face-aid. Pity you can't speak to her as
one woman to another. 'As she an 'usband ?

MONA [*faintly*] :

Yes.

BARLEY :

He gave 'em to her, I expect. Men do funny
things. All you've got to do is to say we can't
find 'em.

MONA :

If she suggests coming round . . .

BARLEY :

Five minutes to one ? Tell 'er we'll be
closed. Say Madame always closes to the tick.
Better ! Say you'll come round and see her.

MONA :
Oh ! I couldn't.

BARLEY :
I'll come with you. Take the bull by the 'orns. You leave it to me when we get there.

MONA :
I dread——

BARLEY :
All you've got to do is to sound a bit breathless. [*Goes to the telephone.*] 'Allo ! Madame Lila's speakin'. . . . 'Old the line. [*To* MONA] Come on – breathless. [*She takes the line from him.*]

MONA :
I – I've looked and asked everywhere, Madam. No sign of them. . . . No, Madam. . . . No. It's just closing time. . . . [BARLEY *prompts her with a nudge and a shake of the head.*] We have to close sharp by law. Would – would [*again* BARLEY *nudges her and nods*] – you like me and the head assistant to come round and see you instead——— ?

BARLEY [*sotto voce*] :
At once.

MONA :
At once. . . . Certainly, Madam ; a pleasure, Madam. . . . No trouble, Madam. . . .

6   73

404 Albert Hall Palace Court Mansions ; yes, Madam. [*Replaces the receiver.*]

BARLEY :

'Albert 'All Palace Court Mansions' – the poor fish ! [*He regards* MONA, *who is leaning against the wall with her eyes closed.*] Cheerio – you did that well. The thing is to give the impression that we're more anxious to get 'em back than she is 'erself. No pretence there – they're bound to be insured for more than they're worth. Come back 'ere, and mind you put on a soupson o' sunburn, an' touch up your lips.

MONA :

I shall never go through with it, Mr. Barley.

BARLEY :

Oh, yes, you will ! We'll stop at Smart's an' get you a dose o' sal volatile. That'll buck you up. [*He pats her shoulder.*] Put a face on it.

MONA *covers her lips with her hand, and goes out.*

BARLEY *busies himself with the putting to rights of his department – singing,* " *They've a colour like the rose – but when that colour goes – 'ow different they look by light o' day.*"

Girls ! She 'asn't got the brass of most of 'em nowadays.

74

*He washes his hands and takes up a hand
mirror to make sure that his toothbrush moustaches stop exactly at the corners of his lips, takes
a razor and squares the hair at the ears ; slips
off his apron, and dons his jacket and billycock
hat, then closes the shop door. He is now ready,
and takes up the paper.*

I shall 'ave a bob on those two both ways. Now
where's that girl ? [*Calling*] Miss Curtis !
Oh ! 'Ere you are ! That's better. Now
remember ; she don't know a thing ; just
make a straight lip of it. Keep it off yourself,
and on to the establishment – impersonal.
Remember I'm the boss in Madame Lila's
absence. Shove it on to me. Other girl gone ?
[MONA *nods.*] And all closed ? [MONA *nods.*]
Well, we'll go out at the back. Mind, the first
you knew of it was 'er ringing up this morning ;
and whatever you say, stick to it. You can't go
pale in that complexion, can you ?

MONA :
I could faint in it.

BARLEY :
Well, don't ! Unless you'd like to get it
over before we start. [*There is the sound of a taxi
stopping, and the ring of a bell.* MONA *gives a
gasp.* BARLEY *sidesteps to the shop right and
squints round.*]

75

BARLEY [*nodding – in a whisper*] :
Can't see. Lucky we'd gone. [*The bell rings again.*] Ring away !

MONA [*whispering*] :
She can't see in, can she ?

BARLEY :
Nao ; but we'd better wait. 'Ere, stand straight ! Catch 'old o' my shoulder. [*There is a sharp tapping on the door.*] Knock away. When a shop's shut, it *is* shut.

MONA :
Hadn't we better open and get it over ?

BARLEY :
And throw away the good impression ? She's bound to go back and wait for us. We'll be there almost before her. Supposin' it *is* 'er carryin' on outside. Besides, you've got to 'ave that dope. [*Once more the bell is rung, and there is a sharp tapping.*]

MONA [*gasping – her nerves all ragged*] :
Oh ! Hell !

BARLEY :
That's better ! But that's the last time, you'll see.

> *Both listen. There is the sound of a taxi starting.*

76

BARLEY :

Right away ! We can go now. [*Looking at the clock*] She only missed us by a minute and an 'alf. We'll get that dope, take a bus, and be there in a quarter of an hour. What's she want these pearls for in such an 'urry ? Looks as if they really was reel. On the other 'and, if they was, she'd rather 'ave the value.

MONA :

They were real.

BARLEY :

'Ow do you know ? You never 'ad any.

MONA :

It's the feel.

BARLEY :

Fiddle ! Come along, my girl !

He leads towards the door on the left. MONA *takes a long breath, braces herself, and follows.*

ACT II

SCENE I

The LEPPEDGES' *flat in Albert Hall Palace Court Mansions; a tastefully furnished green-panelled room ; twelve forty-five on the same morning.* HELEN LEPPEDGE, *a well-built nicely preserved young woman, is standing by the telephone.*

HELEN :
No ; all the better. And you ? . . . Good. . . . I say, do you remember if I had any pearls on last night ? . . . No ? Damn ! He'll be back before lunch. He always notices little things, especially when he's given them to me. . . . Yes, darling ; but could you possibly go round to Paulati's, or telephone, asking whether they've been picked up ? And would you look round at home ? That would be frightfully nice of you. And would you phone me ? . . . Oh ! And if it should be a male voice, ask his number and say it's the wrong one. . . . Wasn't it divine ? . . .

ARTHUR LEPPEDGE, *about forty years old, of square and substantial build, stands listening.*

HELEN [*noticing*] :
Well, good-bye, darling. [*Cuts off.*]

78

ARTHUR :
  What's divine ?

HELEN :
  A dress at Jay's we saw yesterday.

ARTHUR :
  And who is a darling ?

HELEN :
  Maud.   Aren't you a bit early ?

ARTHUR :
  Tubby drove me up.

HELEN :
  Anybody try to vamp you at Maidenhead ?

ARTHUR [*approaching her*] :
  You're looking very fresh.   Give me a kiss.

HELEN [*holding up a creamy cheek*] :
  I do dislike cigary kisses.

ARTHUR :
  What's happened to your neck ?

HELEN :
  Nothing.

ARTHUR [*with his head on one side and a round
    eye*] :
  Pearls ?

HELEN :
  Yes ; I've mislaid them.

79

ARTHUR :

You've——— !

HELEN :

Don't get in a stew, because that'll be two stews in one morning.

ARTHUR :

Mislaid ? How d'you mean – lost ?

HELEN :

For the moment.

ARTHUR :

Do you know they cost about twelve hundred ?

HELEN :

Awful, isn't it ?

ARTHUR :

When did you miss them ?

HELEN :

I don't really know. I don't seem to remember them one way or the other till I got up this morning. You don't – little things you wear every day.

ARTHUR :

When was the last time you noticed the pearls yesterday ?

HELEN :

Well, if I had them on, I must have had them off at the hairdresser's.

ARTHUR :
  Why ?

HELEN :
  Because I had my neck done.

ARTHUR :
  When ?

HELEN :
  About tea-time.

ARTHUR :
  You mean you can't remember whether you
had them on at all yesterday ?

HELEN :
  I'm pretty sure I had them on till I went to
the hairdresser's.

ARTHUR :
  Have you asked there ?

HELEN :
  I was just going to get them.   I've only been
out of bed half an hour.

ARTHUR :
  Taking it out.

HELEN :
  Yes ; I had a tremendous dissipation.

ARTHUR :
  What ?

HELEN :

Prom – all English composers.   Most emotionalising.

ARTHUR :

Try the Queen's Hall, then.

HELEN [*dialling*] :

There's that high buzzing.

ARTHUR :

Replace the receiver.

HELEN [*languidly*] :

London's just full of people shooting grouse and ringing up the Queen's Hall.   [*Dialling again*] Yes. . . . Is that the Queen's Hall ? Can you tell me, please, if a pearl necklace has been picked up from last night ?   I was sitting in the Grand Circle, row three, near the centre. . . . Nothing at all picked up ? . . . You're sure. Thank you.   [*To her husband*] They must get that answer by heart.

ARTHUR :

Did you try a dress on at Jay's ?

HELEN :

No.   We were looking at advance models.

ARTHUR :

And from there, where did you go ?

HELEN :

Straight to the hairdresser's.

ARTHUR :

Well, get *them*. [HELEN *looks for the number*.] Seems to me you make very light of those pearls.

HELEN [*with a faint mockery*] :

Oh ! no, darling. [*Dialling*] Is that Madame Lila's ? . . . Mrs. Leppedge speaking. . . . Is Madame Lila in ? . . . Will she be long ? . . . Who is speaking ? . . . I see. I should like to speak to the girl who did my face and neck yesterday, please. [*A longish wait, during which* ARTHUR *comes closer*.] Is that Miss Curtis ? You remember doing my neck yesterday. I've missed my pearls. . . . I was wondering whether I left them. . . . They must have been off my neck when it was being done. . . . No, I don't. But if you remember taking them off. . . . I think I must have left them. . . . Kensington eight o, double o, o.

ARTHUR :

What's her voice like ?

HELEN :

Quavery.

ARTHUR :

What's she doing now ?

HELEN :

Having a look round.

ARTHUR :

Or pretending to be.

HELEN :

Arthur, you are horrid.

ARTHUR :

Well, why should she quaver ?

HELEN :

You'd quaver if someone were suspecting you of cheating at cards.

ARTHUR :

Oh ! bosh ! Look here, say you'll come round.

HELEN [*into the mouthpiece*] :

No. . . . Madame Lila's not come in ? . . . And you say she won't be back ? Early closing. . . . Yes, that will do perfectly. . . . You're sure it's not troubling you ? . . . My address is 404 Albert Hall Palace Court Mansions. [*She replaces the receiver.*]

ARTHUR :

What's that ?

HELEN :

She and the chief man assistant are coming round.

ARTHUR :

Why should they, unless they're putting up a bluff ? If I were you I'd jump into a taxi ; you'd be there by one.

HELEN :
Oh, no ! I must wait for them, now.

ARTHUR :
I don't see — if you're slippy.

HELEN [*decidedly*] :
No. [*A thought strikes her.*] *You* go, and say
I sent you, to save them the trouble. It's your
funeral.

ARTHUR :
Mine ! H'm ! Well, I *will* go.

HELEN :
Good, darling ! I'm sure you're wise.

ARTHUR *gives her a look, as if saying " I
never know where you're getting off," and goes
out.*

HELEN [*quietly*] :
Thank God ! [*Opens the door an inch, listens
for the clang of the lift door ; goes to the telephone
and dials.*] Hallo ? Yes. . . . Any news of the
pearls ? . . . No ? Oh ! . . . He's back ; full
of hearty Maidenhead air — but I've got him on
the run for the moment. I wanted to save you
lying on the phone. The P.M.G. doesn't like
it. Neither lying nor love-making ; he has
good principles. . . . Yes, darling, but I *said*
he had. . . . You realised that the last " darling,"
when I cut off before, wasn't for you. . . . You

85

can't imagine how quick he was noticing the undisguised purity of my neck. . . . Well, as a fact, he's running about London at the moment seeing impurities everywhere. . . . Yes, but, what I was going to say was : This is going to take me all my time ; and if I don't get them back it's going to take me still more time. So everything's off until I phone you again. . . . Abso*lute*ly, darling. . . . But abso-*lute*ly, bless you ! [*She makes the sound of a kiss with her lips and touches them with her finger.*] [*To herself*] How perfectly marvellous it will be when you can see by television how he looks when you blow him a kiss ! Only, will he – by then ? [*Aware that the door has been opened.*]

WALSH :
 At what time lunch, Madam ?

HELEN :
 Well, Walsh, what with one thing and another, I should say – two-ish.

WALSH :
 Then I'd better call the soufflé off, Madam.

HELEN :
 Yes.   But bring in some sherry – four glasses.

WALSH :
 The old sherry, Madam ?

86

HELEN [*with a smile*] :

Unless there's any older. How melancholy it is that one dies before sherry's fit to drink.

WALSH :

Yes, Madam.

HELEN :

My grandfather always sent his best sherry to the West Indies for at least two voyages ; but I never knew whether being rolled about made it less or more yellow.

WALSH :

Being rolled about, Madam ?

HELEN :

And you've got to allow for the cask – I think they were rum casks – a sort of pickling. I feel that to be rolled about in a rum cask would have a distinct effect on me. [WALSH *giggles*.] By the way, had you realised that I've got no pearls on ?

WALSH :

Yes, Madam.

HELEN :

How wonderful you are ! Well, where are they ? You haven't put them anywhere safe ?

WALSH :

Next the skin for pearls, Madam, is safest.

HELEN :

That's what I think, day after day.

WALSH :

No one can't get at them there.

HELEN :

Not while one's morals are sound.

WALSH :

Madam ?

HELEN :

Um – are there any salted almonds left ?

WALSH :

Yes, Madam.

HELEN :

Bring those too, then. They steady the mental *tempo*.

> WALSH *smiles and goes out.* HELEN *stands with her head on one side, thinking.*

HELEN :

Yes, next the skin *is* safest. [*She goes to her writing-bureau, unlocks a shallow drawer, and takes out a sheet of paper. Reading it through, and slipping it down her dress*] Safe there, unless Arthur ravishes me.

> WALSH *returns with the sherry and four glasses ; also salted almonds on a salver.*

HELEN :

Can you remember seeing my pearls when I came in yesterday afternoon ?

WALSH :

Can't say I can, Madam.

HELEN :

Or when I went out to dinner ?

WALSH :

No, Madam.

HELEN :

They seem to lie between the hairdresser's
and the taxi, then. How does one get hold
of a taxi that drove one here from a hairdresser's
in High Street about six o'clock ?

WALSH :

Did you take it off a stand ?

HELEN :

Yes.

WALSH :

Notice anything about him, Madam ?

HELEN :

A Hitler moustache.

WALSH :

Ah ! Then I've seen him when I've been
coming out of Kensington Gardens. I think
he has his afternoon nap at the keb rank there.
Shall I ring up that rank, Madam ?

HELEN :

Please, Walsh. Use your well-known
discretion.

WALSH *smiles, goes to the telephone, and
dials.*

WALSH :

Hallo ! [*A faint answering* " Alloo ! " *permeates the room.*] That the keb rank ? Have you any keb on the rank ? [*Faint* " Nao."] Do you know a kebman with a Charlie Chaplin moustache ? [*Faint* " Nao – Oaw ! You mean Chawlie ! "] Well, listen – when he comes on the rank for lunch send him straight off to 404 Elbert Hall Pelece Court Mansions, where he brought a lady to yesterday afternoon about six, from a hairdresser's in the 'Igh ; 404 – got that ? A Charlie Chaplin moustache. [*Faint* " Right-o ! "] Very faithful to their stand, Ma'am.

HELEN :

Marvellous, Walsh ! [*The door is opened and* ARTHUR *comes in.*] Well ?

ARTHUR :

Drew blank. [WALSH *slides out.*] Have you asked *her* ?

HELEN :

I think we've treed the cabman who brought me back here.

ARTHUR :

How ?

HELEN :

By his resemblance to Hitler.

ARTHUR :
Blasted half-toothbrush ?

HELEN :
When he comes on to his stand, he's to come round.

ARTHUR :
What's this sherry for ?

HELEN [*taking up a glass*] :
I shall want my lunch before I get it.

ARTHUR :
I want mine now. [*Takes up another glass. The two sip and nibble.*] So you had a beano last night ?

HELEN [*scenting awkward questions*] :
Yes. Who was down at Tubby's ?

ARTHUR :
Oh ! Nobody.

HELEN :
Who were the others ? Who's Mrs. Tubby at the moment ?

ARTHUR :
He keeps her very dark.

HELEN :
It's that little fair thing, Dorothy Somer. Was she there ?

ARTHUR :

No. I mean – yes. But it's not her.

HELEN :

Did she tell you ?

ARTHUR :

Well, as a fact—— [*Lights a cigarette.*]
Have one ? [HELEN *shakes her head with a
smile.*] As a fact——

HELEN :

You've said that, my dear. No confessions.

ARTHUR :

Confessions ? I—— !

HELEN :

You know the word.

ARTHUR :

But look here——

HELEN :

That's quite enough.

ARTHUR :

D'you mean to say that because I said " As
a fact "——

HELEN :

Twice ; and didn't contradict it.

ARTHUR :

Really, Helen, I wish you'd be serious.

92

HELEN :
To be serious leads to all sorts of. . . divorce.
Well, who else was there ?

ARTHUR [*sulkily*] :
I'm not a rubber-neck conductor.

HELEN [*head to one side*] :
Straight before you — Mr. Tubby Cart-
wright, fine old specimen of Georgian archi-
tecture, wearing thin on the top story. To
his left, that delicate piece——

ARTHUR :
Shut up !

HELEN :
Isn't she a " piece " ? [*The door is opened.*]
Yes ?

WALSH :
A Mr. Barley and a Miss Curtis, Madam.

HELEN :
Quite. Show them in, and cancel the
empty glasses.

WALSH :
Yes, Madam.

> WALSH *goes out.* HELEN *crosses to the fire-*
> *place.* ARTHUR *sulkily regards her.*

> WALSH *returns, ushering in* BARLEY *and*
> MONA.

HELEN :

Very good of you to have come. Will you have some sherry ? Arthur !

They take the glasses handed to them.

BARLEY :

Your 'ealth. [*Tosses off the sherry.*] We thought it better to relieve your minds, seein' it's early closin'. Miss Curtis will give you a rĕsumē.

HELEN :

Yes ?

MONA [*uneasily*] :

Madam, as I told you on the phone——

BARLEY :

That's right.

MONA :

I've looked everywhere, and I'm quite sure they're not in the place.

BARLEY :

'Igh class of customer, ours.

HELEN [*smiling, and raising her eyebrows*] :

That's why we thought they might not be in the place.

BARLEY :

What's that ?

94

HELEN [*suavely*] :

They're not big things, are they, Mr. –
er——

BARLEY :

Barley.

HELEN :

Anybody could slip a handkerchief over
them and spirit them away.

BARLEY :

That's why I came round meself. Miss
Curtis – she's touchy ; and there's two other
girls besides 'er – one of them's on 'er 'oliday.
And Madame Lila – well, you wouldn't expect
Madame. Then there's meself and one other
man assistant at the present time o' speakin'.
Well, you wouldn't expect us, would you ?

HELEN :

I wouldn't expect anyone, Mr. Barley, much
less suspect them.

BARLEY :

Well, what I mean – we can't 'ave our
characters under suspicion ; so I thought
you'd like to give us the once over. They
weren't similes, were they ? [*Fixes his hard
little eyes on* HELEN.]

HELEN [*raising her eyebrows*] :

What do *you* say, Arthur ? Were they
similes ?

ARTHUR :
I paid twelve hundred for them.

BARLEY :
Could I see the insurance policy ?

ARTHUR [*about to say,* " Damn his impu-
    dence ! " *restrains himself, and says*] :
I'll get it. [*He goes out.*]

BARLEY :
In these days nothing seems what it is. It's
never worth goin' out of your way till you've
proved you're dealin' with the original.

HELEN :
Quite true, Mr. Barley.

BARLEY [*mollified*] :
Why should anyone wear originals when
they can get similes for a 'undreth part of the
cost and no one the wiser ? When you 'ave
your pearls stolen these insurance companies
'ave to pay up, because they can't prove to
your satisfaction that you 'adn't lost the
originals.

HELEN :
I was going to ask you, Mr. Barley, how
you prove to their satisfaction that you have ?

BARLEY [*taken aback*] :
Well, you 'ave to allow for each other. Not
that I'd allow much for an insurance company.

You've got their policy, and you 'aven't got the pearls. That's your case.

HELEN :

I'll explain that to my husband ; it seems simple.

BARLEY :

So it is, if you prefer the money. Depends on your 'usband. If you can get your 'usband to give you a string o' pearls every birthday, you've got a steady income ; and you can go about in similes all the time, and no one the wiser.

> ARTHUR *returns, with a paper in his hand. He hands it to* BARLEY, *and turns suddenly to* MONA.

ARTHUR :

When you're doing a customer's face and neck – where do you lay the things down ?

BARLEY [*by way of giving her time*] :

Where do you ?

MONA :

On the little table along the wall. There's a tray.

BARLEY :

A receptacle.

ARTHUR :

What makes you think you laid them down there yesterday ?

MONA :
  I always do.

HELEN :
  Any ear-rings ?

MONA :
  No, Madam ; only those you've got on, and they were so tiny.

HELEN :
  I didn't see any other girl yesterday.

BARLEY :
  There *is* another girl.

MONA :
  She'd gone.   We're so slack, Madam.

HELEN :
  What makes you think I had them on at all ?

MONA :
  Well, really, Madam, I don't know – I seem to remember seeing them.

BARLEY :
  That's right.   You can't speak to things you 'aven't noticed.   The truth's the truth, and beyond that you can't go.

ARTHUR :
  I had a sort of idea you could.

BARLEY :
  'Ow's that ?

98

HELEN :
Well, you've just been saying, Mr. Barley, that nothing is really what it looks like.

MONA [*slightly hysterical*] :
If you don't believe me——

BARLEY :
Now, now ! Of course they believe you. I'm the chief assistant ; anyone that doesn't believe you has got me to deal with.

MONA :
I got nothing but my word——

BARLEY :
Good enough for me is good enough for anybody. We're an 'igh-class concern.

WALSH *enters.*

WALSH :
The driver, Madam.

ARTHUR :
Bring him in.

HELEN :
Some more sherry, Walsh. Would you like another glass, Mr. Barley ?

BARLEY :
Never refuse good stuff.

WALSH *takes out the salver.*

99

ARTHUR :

We shall get to the bottom of it now. Were you still in the shop when I came a few minutes ago ?

BARLEY [*shaking his head*] :

I should say we'd just gone out. Once we're shut, we're shut.

> WALSH *enters with the salver and sherry and three glasses.*

HELEN [*handing* BARLEY *a glass*] :

Not a simile – this, Mr. Barley ?

BARLEY :

Good 'ealth. [*Tosses it off. To* MONA] Why don't you drink yours ?

> MONA *drinks her sherry.*

WALSH [*at the door*] :

Mr. Cadgman.

> *Enter the* TAXI-DRIVER, *who wears a rigid little patch of dark hair square below his nose.*

HELEN [*recognising him*] :

You drove me home here yesterday, didn't you ?

CADGMAN :

That's right, Ma'am, now I see you.

HELEN :

Will you——? [*Hands him a glass.*]

100

CADGMAN :

Thank you. [*Looks around him and tosses it off.*]

ARTHUR :

You know what we want you for ?

CADGMAN :

Not an idea.

ARTHUR :

What do you do with things you pick up in your cab ?

CADGMAN :

Things I pick up ? Take 'em to Scotland Yard. But I don't pick up a thing in a blue moon.

ARTHUR :

Didn't pick up a string of pearls yesterday ?

CADGMAN :

Pearls ? Last time I picked up pearls, they was worth seven and six — so they told me at the Yard. Nobody claimed 'em, so I 'ad my trouble for nothing.

HELEN :

There was nothing left in the cab after you brought me here ?

CADGMAN :

Well, nothing in 'er when I took 'er 'ome.

ARTHUR :
  You looked her over ?
CADGMAN :
  I did ; from top to bottom, and shook the
floor-rug. Not a thing.
HELEN :
  Can you remember your next fare after me ?
CADGMAN :
  Very well ; I didn't 'ave none.
ARTHUR :
  None ?
CADGMAN :
  None. I'd promised me girl to take 'er out.
So I just ran the cab back to the garridge,
tuned 'er up, as I said, and came away. Thank
ye, Sir. [*He takes the remaining glass of sherry
from* ARTHUR *and sucks it down.*]
ARTHUR :
  That's that, then.
CADGMAN :
  But I remember your lady well. I've driven
'er before. [*Touches his Hitlerism.*] Before I
'ad this. [*A little loosened by the sherry.*] My
girl seems to think this gives you character.
BARLEY :
  'Itler's, or Charlie Chaplin's ?
HELEN :
  Both celebrities, Mr. Cadgman.

BARLEY :

If I 'ad them in my shop for ten minutes, they wouldn't be. To think a man can make a name by choppin' the ends off 'is moustache, turnin' out one foot, wearin' a bowler 'at, and treadin' on dogs' tails shows ye what the world is. [*Disputatiously*] Well, if 'e didn't, who'd know 'im from you or me ?

.   .   .   .

1932.